Zoblit Books

The NOT SO Pointless
BLANK JOURNAL

A Create - It - Yourself

The Pointless Blank Journal

A Balanced diet publication

This is a monographic publication.
Apologies for those people who were expecting this Journal Book to be completely blank.
This is not the case. As the author of this book
I wish to inspire you to get writing on a single topic or issue.
We would like all participants to define a starting and an end point which can become
your overall goal to achieve. Whatever you decide to write about should be on a one-off basis.

YES THIS IS A BLANK POINTLESS JOURNAL BOOK

BY
YAYA NOBODY

Zoblit Books
Published by Zoblit ltd
Zoblit ltd, Unit 2 Vulcan House, Vulcan Road Leicester LE5 3EF
A Division of Nothing
Hoping to open a branch in Mars, Jupiter and the Milky Way Galaxy.

I saw a BBC Programme The Apprentice where they created
a children's book within 24hrs from start to finish.
Then friends of mine challenged me to create
15 books in 15 days and I accepted this challenge in a fun way.

So here is my attempt to create my own books.
Seriously do people really read this small print page?
Book Created by Mr Yaya Nobody
Book Illustrated by M Nobody
COPYRIGHT Yaya Nobody until I become Somebody.
To become somebody I will need to sell 1 million copies of this book.
Blank Pages Design by Yaya Nobody
Seriously you are still reading this page!!!
www.zoblit.com
The publisher does not accept any responsibility in what will be created by users of
this Blank Journal. All rights reserved.
No part of this Blank Journal and especially
the blank pages may not be reproduced. If you do there is nothing
I can do about it. Please do not scan the Blank Pages
or Distribute the Blank Pages within this Journal
without my permission.
Please only purchase authorised edition of this Pointless Blank Journal as
I really do want to sell 1 million copies of this book
and become Mr Somebody. So here is the deal.
You complete all the Blank pages of this Journal
and share this amongst your friend.
If they think the stuff you have written is really good
then why not send your completed journal to
Mr Nobody and if it is really good then who knows
Mr Nobody may be able to publish this for you
and you can also become Mr Somebody.
Isbn: Please insert here once your Journal is published : ....
Printed and bound somewhere in this world.
As there is not enough room to write the ISBN in font size 72 pts
on this page please check the back cover for the official ISBN of this publication

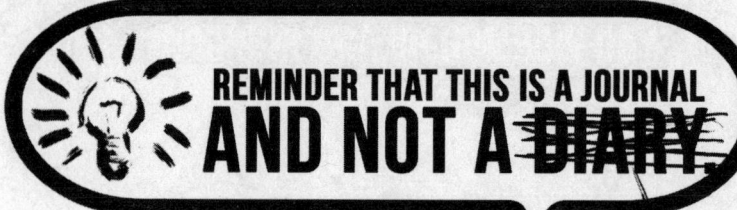

What will be your purpose for using this Journal?

What will be your starting point?

Warning!
The rest of the pages in this Journal are Blank